WHALES

and US

OUR SHARED JOURNEY

India Desjardins
Nathalie Dion

Translated by
David Warriner

ORCA BOOK PUBLISHERS

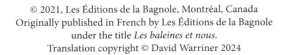

Published in Canada and the United States in 2024 by Orca Book Publishers.
orcabook.com

Library and Archives Canada Cataloguing in Publication
Title: Whales and us : our shared journey / India Desjardins ; [illustrated by] Nathalie Dion ; translated by David Warriner.
Other titles: Baleines et nous. English
Names: Desjardins, India, 1976- author. | Dion, Nathalie, 1964- illustrator. | Warriner, David (Linguist), translator.
Description: Translation of: Les baleines et nous. | Includes index.
Identifiers: Canadiana (print) 20230492134 | Canadiana (ebook) 20230492142 | ISBN 9781459839342 (hardcover) | ISBN 9781459839359 (PDF) | ISBN 9781459839366 (EPUB)
Subjects: LCSH: Whales—Juvenile literature. | LCGFT: Illustrated works.
Classification: LCC QL737.C4 D4713 2024 | DDC j599.5—dc23

Library of Congress Control Number: 2023941592

Summary: This beautifully illustrated nonfiction picture book examines the history, environment, biology and behaviors of whales. Using stories and legends, *Whales and Us* explores humans' relationships to whales, threats to the whales' existence and what we can do to protect them.

Orca Book Publishers is committed to reducing the consumption of nonrenewable resources in the production of our books. We make every effort to use materials that support a sustainable future.

Orca Book Publishers gratefully acknowledges the support for its publishing programs provided by the following agencies: the Government of Canada, the Canada Council for the Arts and the Province of British Columbia through the BC Arts Council and the Book Publishing Tax Credit.

Artwork created using digital watercolor brushes in Photoshop.

Cover and interior artwork by Nathalie Dion
Translated by David Warriner

Printed and bound in South Korea.

27 26 25 24 • 1 2 3 4

WHALES FASCINATE ME. Maybe it's because they're such immense creatures. Maybe it's the way they glide effortlessly through the water. Or maybe it's the sounds they make when they sing, or how smart they are. There's something majestic about them. And there's something so mysterious about the marine world they live in.

For a long time I thought there was no way to explain my obsession with whales. I figured it was something that was just there within me for no reason. Every year I travel to a place called Les Bergeronnes, north of the village of Tadoussac, in Quebec. Here you can watch whales right from the shore, while sitting on the rocks. One day, as I was looking out to where the water meets the horizon, hoping to see a whale breach the shimmering surface, I had a moment of clarity.

I used to come here and see the whales when I was little, and there were dozens of them. I could see them leaping out of the water. I could see their spouts, and their tails slapping the surface. Now I feel lucky if I get to see just one whale's back cresting the waves in the distance. Sitting here one day I realized why whales fascinate me so much. It's because they're like messengers, here to tell us that the world they live in might not last forever.

I'm not a scientist or a whale expert, but I've read and heard a lot of stories about whales during my life. I wanted to share these stories and use them to help people learn more about whales. This is one way for me to pay tribute to these amazing creatures…because one day they might not be here anymore.

India

WHALE OR CETACEAN?

Cetacean is the scientific name for any of the marine mammals in the group that includes whales, porpoises and dolphins. It comes from the Latin word *cetus*, which means "any large sea creature," and from the ancient Greek word Κῆτος (*kētos*), which means "sea monster."

There are two main
groups of cetaceans,
baleen whales and
toothed whales.

1

BALEEN WHALES

Baleen is a series of rigid plates and bristles attached to the upper jaw. Whales use baleen plates to filter water and trap their prey.

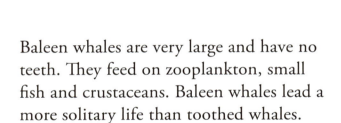

BALEEN ——— DIVER

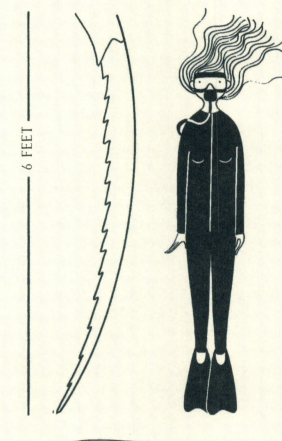

6 FEET

Baleen whales are very large and have no teeth. They feed on zooplankton, small fish and crustaceans. Baleen whales lead a more solitary life than toothed whales.

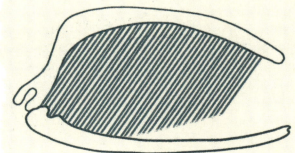

BLUE WHALE

A Few Types of
BALEEN WHALES

HUMPBACK WHALE

MINKE WHALE

FIN WHALE

RIGHT WHALE

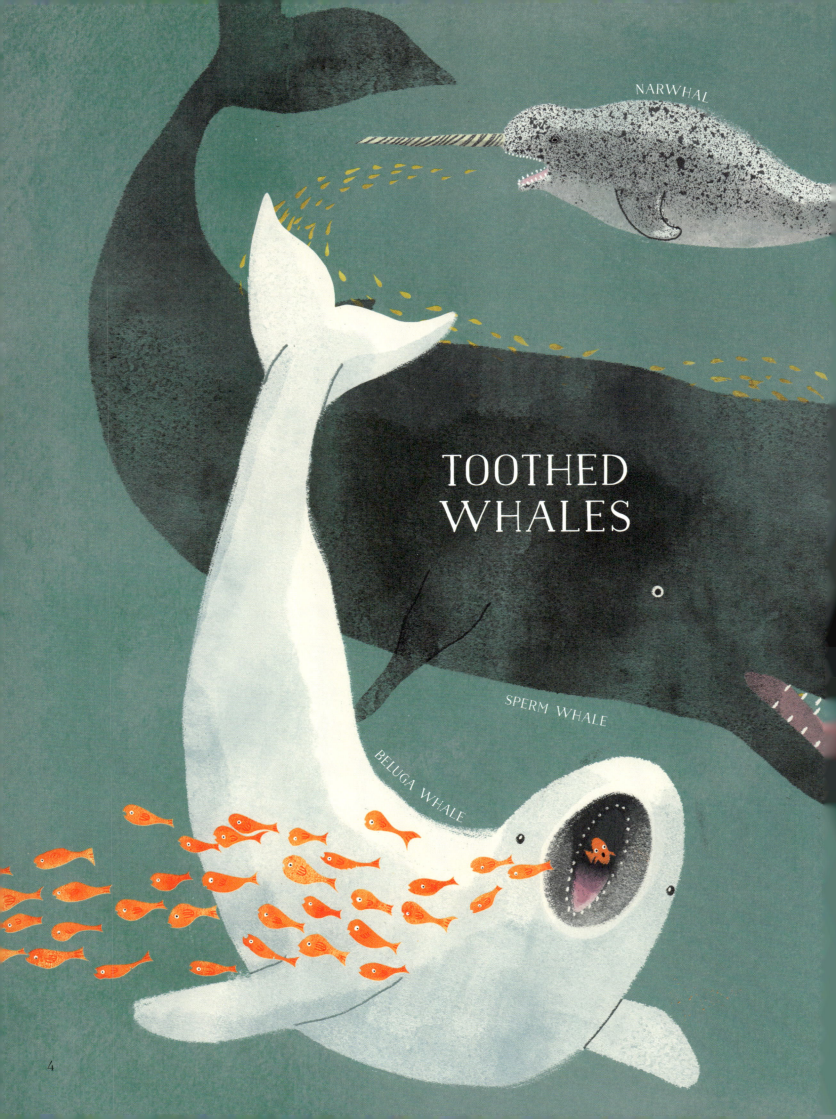

NARWHAL

TOOTHED
WHALES

SPERM WHALE

BELUGA WHALE

4

DOLPHIN

Toothed whales use sound waves and echoes in a process called *echolocation* to communicate and navigate. They feed on larger prey, like fish and squid, which they catch with their teeth and swallow whole. Toothed whales are more social than baleen whales. They live in groups called *pods*.

A Few Types of TOOTHED WHALES

ORCA

SEAL

Whales are not the only marine mammals in the ocean. Here are some others.

SEA LION

WALRUS

MANATEE

SEA OTTER

BLUBBER

MUSCLE

SKIN

BLOOD VESSELS

A LITTLE BIT OF HISTORY

SURVIVAL

Whales have existed for 35 million years. They're huge creatures. But they've only been this big for the last 4.5 million years, and the ice age might have something to do with it. Whales have a layer of fat called *blubber* that keeps them warm, and only those with the most blubber to protect against the cold were able to survive. It's thanks to their blubber that whales were able to migrate longer distances and adapt to different climates.

In addition, the bigger whales were, the easier it was for them to dive for their food. So if you've ever wondered why whales are such an impressive size, it's because of evolution. The survival of the species depended on it.

WHALES…WITH LEGS?

The prehistoric ancestors of cetaceans were land mammals. They had four legs and walked on land. They ate fish and crustaceans. Over millions of years, their bodies evolved. Their legs grew shorter. Their snouts grew longer. And their nostrils moved to a different place on the body to make it easier to breathe underwater. Some whales still have traces of their land-based ancestors, such as pelvic bones and leg bones.

Whether they're scientists or casual observers, people who
spend time with whales always have fascinating stories to tell
about their interactions with them. Some of these stories have
evolved into legends that whale lovers like to share. There's one
story I've heard that I love to tell time and time again. It's so
amazing that people sometimes don't know whether to believe it.

AN UNFORGETTABLE ENCOUNTER

One day a fisherman saw a beluga caught in a fishing net near the shore. It was trying to escape, but it was really stuck. The tide started to come in, and at first the beluga could still lift its head out of the water to breathe. But soon the water was too deep for the beluga to reach the surface.

The fisherman came closer and tried to free the beluga from the net. He managed to cut away one side of the net with a knife, but the beluga was still unable to swim free.

Luckily the fisherman was also a diver. He put on his diving gear and went underwater to untangle the net. The currents and the rising tide made this a very difficult thing to do. What's more, the beluga was afraid and distressed. But eventually the fisherman was able to untangle the knots in the net and set the beluga free.

The terrified beluga swam away as quickly as it could. Then suddenly it stopped and turned around. It swam back toward the shore, toward the fisherman, and they stared at each other for a long moment. Then the beluga gave a nod of its head and swam off again.

Every time the fisherman told this story, people would ask, "Why did the beluga come back?"

And he would reply, "I think it wanted to say thank you."

COULD THIS FISHERMAN'S STORY BE TRUE?

WHY DO WHALES NEED AIR TO BREATHE?

Whales are mammals. They have lungs, so they need air to breathe. They breathe through giant nostrils called *blowholes* on the top of their heads. Toothed whales have one blowhole, and baleen whales have two. Powerful muscles stop the water from getting in.

When whales breach the surface, they open their blowholes and push out a mixture of air and water droplets. That's what we call a whale's *spout*. The warm air condenses, like steam or a cloud, when it comes into contact with the cold air outside.

While breathing is automatic for humans, it's something whales have to do consciously. But when humans swim underwater, we do the same things that whales do. We breathe in before diving under the surface, come back up when we need to breathe out, then take in more air.

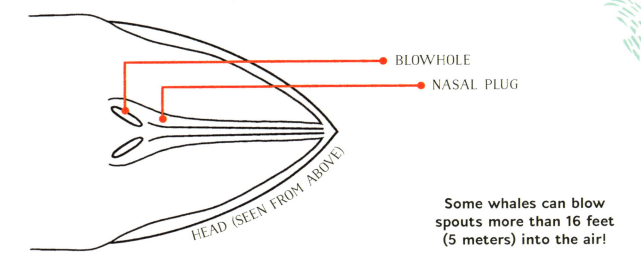

BLOWHOLE

NASAL PLUG

HEAD (SEEN FROM ABOVE)

Some whales can blow spouts more than 16 feet (5 meters) into the air!

FISHING NETS

Every year many cetaceans get caught in fishing nets. They often drown or starve to death because they can't swim free or come up to the surface to breathe. It can be very risky for humans to try to rescue them. Divers who try to save a stuck whale can put themselves in danger too. That's why, if you see a whale in distress, it's best to call the emergency services. Unfortunately there's only so much that marine rescuers can do because their resources are limited, and too many whales end up losing their lives caught in a net.

CAN WHALES NOD THEIR HEADS?

Unlike most other cetaceans, the beluga has a very flexible neck. That means it can move its head in ways that many other species of whales can't.

WHY DO WHALES SWIM SO CLOSE TO SHORE?

There are several reasons why whales might come close to land. When the water near the shore is deep, it can make it easier for whales to feed. They can trap their prey against the rocks underwater. Whales are also naturally curious creatures, so maybe they like to swim near the shore to see what's happening.

CAN WHALES SHOW GRATITUDE?

Rescued whales have sometimes been seen leaping out of the water or swimming closer to their rescuers, but we don't really know why. Some think it's the whales' way of saying thank you, and scientists are doing research to see if that's true. But others are cautious about interpreting animal behavior based on our understanding of human behavior. They think we should learn more about how whales communicate before we assume anything.

HOW WHALES COMMUNICATE

THE MYTH OF THE SIREN'S SONG

For hundreds of years, myths and legends have told how sailors and fearsome pirates have perished at sea, lured by the sound of a siren's song. We've all heard the stories—the siren's song is so enchanting, it draws seafarers irresistibly into the depths of the ocean, never to be seen again.

Could the myth of the siren's song be inspired by whale sounds? Maybe, but because we don't know for certain where myths come from, it's hard to say for sure.

WHALE SONG

What we call "whale song" is actually a series of sounds, repeated over and over. Baleen whales—especially male humpback whales—make these sounds during the mating season. This kind of whale song is thought to have something to do with attracting a mate. Other kinds of whale songs might be connected to navigation and feeding. More studies are needed before we can really understand, but researchers have found that some repetitions and variations can be shared between territories and passed down from one generation to the next.

Toothed cetaceans, like beluga whales and dolphins, make different types of sounds. They use a series of whistles and clicks for communication and echolocation. Some scientists are doing research to interpret these sounds in the hope that humans and whales will be able to communicate one day. But others are critical of this research. They think that we should not be using a human frame of reference to try to make sense of whale sounds.

To understand how whales communicate, we should not analyze their language by trying to translate it and make it fit into the way humans see the world. Instead we should try to understand their language based on how it fits into their own world.

RADIO BUOY

HYDROPHONE

17

SOUNDS

Baleen whales produce sound inside their larynx and transmit it through other organs, such as their lungs and sinuses.

LARYNGEAL SAC

LUNGS

BLOWHOLE

Toothed whales make clicking and whistling sounds using special organs inside their heads called phonic lips.

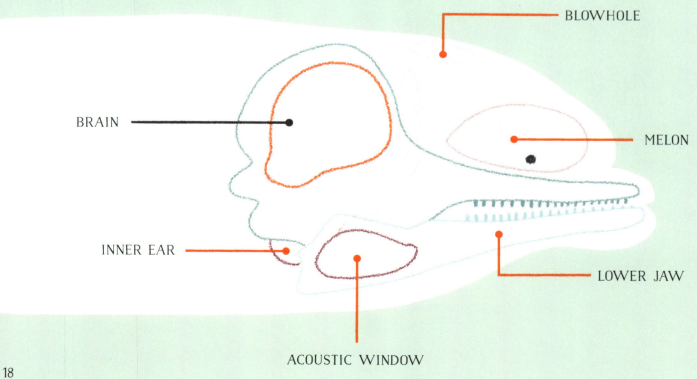

BLOWHOLE

BRAIN

MELON

INNER EAR

LOWER JAW

ACOUSTIC WINDOW

ECHOLOCATION

It's so dark in the depths of the ocean that sound replaces light. Whales use low-frequency sounds to communicate. They send messages to other whales to let them know that there's a boat, a predator or food nearby. These sounds can travel hundreds of miles.

Toothed whales can also emit high-frequency sounds called ultrasound that work like radar to help them locate objects they can't see with their eyes. They send out these sound waves and interpret the way they bounce back to determine the identity and location of an object and how to approach it. This is called *echolocation*.

Belugas and narwhals have the most sophisticated and advanced echolocation systems of all whales.

GIANT TALES

Someone told me the story of a woman who was kayaking on the St. Lawrence River and stopped to take a break beside a rock. Then the rock opened its eye! It wasn't a rock...it was a sperm whale!

ARE WHALES DANGEROUS?

Some might find it surprising that such huge creatures can come so close to humans and pose little risk to us. But attacks by cetaceans are actually very rare. Their ability to assess their environment is so great that when a human is around—paddling in a kayak or diving— they know very well that a person is there and how to steer clear. In other words, if they wanted to attack, they would. And because they're not interested in us as food, they tend to leave us alone.

SPERM WHALES

Sperm whales are the biggest of the toothed whales. Males can grow as long as 50 to 60 feet (15 to 18 meters). They mostly eat fish and squid. For a long time they were hunted for their spermaceti, a white, waxy substance found in an organ inside their heads. At first people thought that sperm whales used this substance for reproduction. Today researchers believe that sperm whales use their spermaceti organ either to control how they float and dive or for echolocation.

CLASSIC WHALE STORIES

Herman Melville's classic novel *Moby-Dick; or, The Whale*, published in 1851, was inspired by a true story. In 1820 the whale-hunting ship *Essex* sank after it was attacked by a sperm whale. The novel tells the story of Captain Ahab, who wants to get revenge on a white sperm whale that bit off his leg. Here's an interesting fact, though—sperm whales are not white. It's thought that the whale that inspired the story must have been an albino.

IS THE STORY REALISTIC?
WOULD A SPERM WHALE REALLY ATTACK A HUMAN?

Well, sperm whales are carnivorous predators with teeth, which they might use to defend themselves. But very few attacks on humans have ever been reported. We're just not that tempting for sperm whales to eat! Events like the one that inspired the story of *Moby-Dick* are believed to happen only when a whale is attacked, which would understandably make the creature behave more aggressively.

In the 1940 Walt Disney animated film *Pinocchio*, Monstro the whale swallows the puppet maker Geppetto and the crew of his boat. Pinocchio then finds the whale and gets swallowed too. He lights a fire inside the beast's belly to make it sneeze, and smoke begins to rise from its blowhole. When the whale finally sneezes, it blows them all out to sea through its mouth.

This story is very imaginative but not at all realistic. A whale's blowhole is not connected to its stomach. So things inside the stomach, like smoke from the fire Pinocchio started, can't flow out of its blowhole.

What kind of whale was Monstro supposed to be? Monstro has teeth, so it was probably supposed to be a sperm whale, like the whale in *Moby-Dick*. In some images, Monstro looks more like a blue whale, but blue whales don't have teeth. Plus, no matter how big blue whales grow, their stomachs are far too small to contain even one human.

WHALE HUNTING

Since 1986 whale hunting has been strictly regulated around the world. Commercial whaling is banned almost everywhere, but some countries continue to do it. Other countries claim to hunt whales for scientific research. But some people doubt that's true, because many of the whales that are hunted end up being sold for their meat.

HOW LONG HAVE PEOPLE HUNTED WHALES?

The Basque people in Europe started hunting whales in the ninth century.
Sperm whales especially were hunted for their spermaceti, which was used
as a lubricant for machines and burned in oil lamps. Several other species
of whales were also highly prized for their blubber and their meat.

WHALE TOURISM

"This is where whale tourism started!" said Dominique, a man who's passionate about whales. Every year he goes to watch whales in the small community of Les Bergeronnes.

He told me how in 1975 a whale was stranded on the shore of the St. Lawrence, not far from his home. At the time there weren't many resources to deal with something so big. And because it takes just a few days for a dead whale to start smelling really bad, the people in the village knew they had to act fast. They called in people from outside the village to help. They had to cut the whale carcass into pieces and truck it all away to the city, where some pieces were turned into animal feed and others taken to the dump. It took about a week to clean up the shore after the whale was beached.

During that time a group of European tourists was visiting the area. They got to see the beached whale and the cleanup mission that followed. The tourists were fascinated and came back each day to watch. At the end of their vacation, they went home. Soon after that people in the community started to see more and more curious tourists. "We heard there were whales in the area," they would say.

At that time fishing was the only way for people in the area to earn a living. The fishermen started to invite tourists aboard their boats, saying they sometimes saw whales while they were fishing. They took tourists out for hours at a time to enjoy the water and hopefully see one of these gigantic creatures. Gradually the word began to spread. More and more tourists came to visit, and the fishermen figured they could charge a small amount of money to take them aboard. Little by little, whale-watching tours became a thing, and a whole tourism industry has grown out of it.

THE STORIES AND THE FACTS

Stories about whale tourism can be just as interesting as stories about the creatures themselves. Whale tourism is thought to date back to the late 1940s and 1950s in California, when students at the Scripps Institution of Oceanography in San Diego began carrying out annual counts of gray whales. In 1950 a nearby monument was converted into a public whale-watching lookout, attracting thousands of people. Then, in 1955, a San Diego fisherman started charging $1 for people to observe whales from his boat, and this set in motion a wave of business opportunities.

The first whale-watching operations in North America started up in 1971, when the Zoological Society of Montreal offered members of the public the chance to observe fin whales, minke whales and beluga whales in the St. Lawrence River. But it was only in the 1980s, once a general ban on commercial whaling was announced, that whale watching really became a popular activity.

- Whale-watching tours are run in 119 countries around the world.

- Each year more than 13 million people go out to observe marine mammals in their natural habitat.

- This industry generates about $2.1 billion every year and brings significant economic benefits to local communities.

29

WHY DO SOME WHALES GET STRANDED?

NATURAL CAUSES

Accidents happen. Some whales find themselves beached in shallow waters where the ocean floor slopes gently. They swim close to shore and get stuck. They might venture into shallow water by mistake or to flee from a predator, like a shark. Since some whales are sociable creatures that live in pods, if one whale swims into shallow water, the others in the pod may follow. Tides can also explain why whales get beached. When the tide is high, whales can swim a little closer to shore. But when the tide goes out again, they can get stuck if the water gets too shallow for them to swim away.

HUMAN CAUSES

People are another reason why whales get stranded on the shore. It's important not to downplay the impact of human activity. The noise caused by maritime traffic can injure whales and affect their ability to navigate the waters. Some beached whales have been found to have bleeding in the inner ear. This is evidence of acoustic trauma, which is damage to the ear that may cause reduced or lost hearing. If the underwater environment gets too loud, it becomes a problem for whale species that use echolocation to find their way.

CLIMATE CHANGE

Climate change is affecting the marine environment in several ways. It has a negative impact on the populations of zooplankton and crustaceans, which means there's less food for whales. This alone is a threat to their survival. But that's not all. There's also been an increase in toxic algae, which is thought to be spreading as a result of human activity and climate change. Because whales eat algae too, the toxic stuff can be a threat to them.

WHERE DO WHALES LIVE?

It's possible to see whales in many places around the world because they migrate long distances to find food and to reproduce. More recently climate change has influenced their migration patterns as well.

MIGRATION

Whales mate and give birth to their young in warm water, but they feed in cold water. That's why they migrate such long distances. For example, humpback whales can travel more than 2,500 miles (4,000 kilometers) in just over a month, as they migrate between Hawaii, where they spend the winter, and Alaska, where they spend the summer.

HOW CAN WHALES SURVIVE IN DIFFERENT CLIMATES?

Having a thick layer of blubber helps whales migrate a long way and live in different climates. They have evolved to travel great distances and survive in harsh climates, and they still do this today.

A DIFFICULT JOURNEY

It's getting more difficult and dangerous for whales to make their long journeys, due to some of the same reasons why many of them get stranded. Imagine a human mother with her baby, trying to cross a busy street with a blindfold over her eyes and headphones over her ears. With all the noise from maritime traffic, that's what it must be like for whales when they're trying to migrate.

IS WHALE WATCHING HARMFUL TO WHALES?

Despite strict regulations to protect whales, there are still some issues with whale-watching tourism. The noise of the boat engines is stressful for the whales, and more maritime traffic means greater chances of boats colliding with whales.

In some parts of the world where tourism is less tightly regulated, people on cruise ships have been known to feed whales to attract them closer. One danger of this practice is that the creatures may become domesticated and grow so dependent on humans that they lose the capacity to feed themselves.

This type of behavior has caused problems with other species. When wild animals become dependent on humans for food, they can become more aggressive. Eventually, when they don't get the food they need and can no longer fend for themselves, they may turn on nearby humans and attack.

People's expectations are another problem that the whale-watching industry is facing. Tourists want a special experience and to take great photos. They want to see the famous whale tails that advertising has promised. But depending on where people are visiting and the population of whales known to frequent that area, tourists might get only a glimpse of a whale's spout or its back breaching the surface. If people don't see what they expected or don't get the photos they wanted, they can be disappointed. And when people complain, it puts more pressure on the boat captains and encourages some of them to do things that might be harmful to marine life.

SOME CHALLENGES FOR TOURISTS

It can be a challenge for some people to travel mind-
fully and with respect for nature. It's important to
appreciate that whales are free-swimming creatures
that are in their natural habitat, not an aquarium.
As tourists, we have to realize that while we
will see some spectacular scenery, we might
not actually get to see a whale or shoot
a video that's sure to go viral. We have
to be patient and consider ourselves
lucky if we do get to see a whale.
It's a privilege that will forever be
imprinted on our minds.

SOME AMAZING WHALE FACTS

PEOPLE HAVE TOLD ME SOME INCREDIBLE STORIES
ABOUT HOW WHALES HELP OTHERS.

While a shark was attacking a seal, a humpback whale came along and fought off the predator, then carried the seal on its back toward safety.

When a beluga was having trouble because of a deformity in its spine, other whales in its pod were seen swimming alongside to help it along.

DO WHALES REALLY HELP EACH OTHER? AND WOULD THEY REALLY HELP ANOTHER SPECIES?

Most mammals cooperate among themselves to improve their chances of survival. It might be a mother helping her young, or members of the same group helping one another. Experts think this behavior might even be a form of empathy, where an individual takes care of another in difficulty even if that means putting itself in danger.

GRIEF

After studying cetaceans for decades, all around the world, researchers have observed behaviors that make them think whales experience grief and mourn their dead.

Whales have been seen carrying other whales that have died. Researchers have also observed whales that isolated themselves from their group or stopped feeding. Some rescuers have even said that as they removed the carcass of a dead whale, other whales from the pod followed them, sometimes touching the dead whale as they passed, until the water became too shallow for them to swim any farther.

These types of behaviors have been observed mainly in toothed whales, including beluga whales and sperm whales. Researchers believe there haven't been enough studies yet about grief in baleen whales.

INTELLIGENCE

Scientists agree that cetaceans possess a certain form of intelligence when it comes to communication, cooperation and even cultural differences among some species.

CULTURE

Researchers have observed that different groups within a certain species may have different cultures. For example, some groups may have different food preferences or ways of hunting, and some may communicate and express grief differently. In this sense, *culture* refers to things that are passed down from one generation to another.

WHEN WHALES GET LOST

Whales usually stay in big expanses of salt water, but sometimes they lose their way and find themselves in places that are not ideal for their survival.

In May 2020 a humpback whale was found near Montreal, a long way from its natural habitat. It spent its days swimming in the river, slapping its tail on the surface and jumping out of the water. People could also see its spout. A crowd of curious onlookers gathered to watch it.

This was not the first time a whale had been seen near a big city. When this happens there are some things we can do to help the whale find its way home, as long as it's not too far off course. Whale rescuers near San Francisco once helped a mother and her calf make their way to safety. The pair only had to swim about 60 miles (100 kilometers). However, most attempts to help have failed in cases where whales had to travel longer distances to get to safety. The whale that was lost near Montreal was nearly 250 miles (400 kilometers) from home. It would have been risky for humans to intervene, and the chances of a successful rescue operation were slim.

Our relationship to these "sea monsters" has changed a lot over the years. In 2020 most people were sympathetic to the whale's plight. They understood that it was out of its natural environment. They hoped it would find its way home and that scientists would help protect it from danger. But in 1901, a lost whale spotted not far from where the humpback whale was seen in Montreal in 2020 was not so warmly welcomed by people in the city. Newspaper articles dubbed the whale a "monster," and hunters went after it.

Ultimately the lives of both whales came to a tragic end. The whale in 1901 was killed by hunters. The whale in 2020 died as well. Experts suspected that a boat had collided with it, but an autopsy failed to determine the cause of death. It was such an unfortunate fate for these creatures that had simply lost their way.

WHY DO WHALES SWIM SO FAR FROM HOME?

A number of things might explain why whales come so close to urban areas. Underwater noise may be affecting echolocation and their ability to navigate. Or whales may simply be exploring new territories or looking for food. We'll probably never really know.

FRESH WATER AND SALT WATER

Whales are born to live in salt water. During migration, however, they may travel through areas of brackish (only somewhat salty) water or fresh water. They can adapt to these environments for short periods, but if they stay in them for too long, they can develop skin problems such as infections and ulcers. Whales can also have problems finding the food they need in unfamiliar waters.

BREACHING

Most people love seeing whales breach the surface and slap their fins and tails. For a long time these behaviors were thought to be hunting techniques or ways for whales to get rid of parasites. That may be the case, but researchers have discovered that whales may do this to communicate with others in their group when they venture far away or when the underwater noise is too loud.

When, to our gasps of admiration, a humpback whale leaps into the air, what if it's actually trying to send a message to its family in order to find its way home? Like when E.T. in the Steven Spielberg movie says to Elliott, the boy who befriended him, "E.T. phone home."

ECOLOGICAL ISSUES

PROTECT THE LAND

My friend Dominique is a nature lover, and I have him to thank for so many whale stories. He once said to me, "You should write a book about me." In the end, I wrote a book that was inspired by his stories and the passion we share for whales. I couldn't finish this book without writing a little more about Dominique and the huge piece of land he owns in Les Bergeronnes, where we can sit and watch the whales. He bought it when he was 20 years old, and he insists on keeping it pristine.

"I bought this land, but I didn't build the world on it. It's not my place to do that."

Over time he's started to say yes to a few tourists wanting to camp out there and enjoy the view. "Don't breathe a word to anyone," Dominique says to people who tell him they love the place. He's aware of ecological issues and how important it is not to have too many people come visit. He knows that might spoil the place. And more than anything, he knows how important it is to keep nature just the way it is and not betray it by building too much.

One day a group of investors who saw the potential of the site offered him millions of dollars to buy it. Dominique said no. He insists that money will never make him happy and seeing nature ruined would make him unhappy.

Over the years Dominique has seen the whale population change and dwindle. That makes him feel very sad.

I once asked him if his descendants
would share the same convictions as him.
He replied, "I hope so. But I won't
be here to make sure."

THE BIGGEST THREATS

Whales are under threat from many risks. Overfishing has devastated their food supply, and it's left behind too many fishing nets for whales to get caught in. Pollution has made many things in their environment harmful to their health, especially if eaten. Underwater noise and maritime traffic are other dangers, and so is hunting.

There are fewer and fewer whales in the world. Their population has plummeted over the years, and some species are at risk of extinction.

In the last century there were as many as 250,000 blue whales in the world.

Today it's estimated that there are just 10,000 to 25,000 remaining. The reality is even more bleak for North Atlantic right whales. There are only 400 of them left, and their population keeps decreasing.

WHAT CAN WE DO?

Many things are contributing to a decline in marine life. But there are also many things we can do together and individually to help protect it.

- We can reduce maritime traffic by introducing stricter regulations and by buying local when possible. More than 80 percent of goods are transported by container ships. Decreasing maritime traffic would reduce fuel and noise pollution in our oceans and lessen the risk of ships colliding with whales.

- We can take action against overfishing by regulating fishing practices more strictly and adopting concrete policies. Individually we can eat less seafood and choose sustainably sourced fish. This would help reduce the number of whales caught in fishing nets and preserve the species they rely on for food.

- We can limit our use of plastic. Plastic objects and fragments are polluting our oceans and the food chain, which is harmful to marine life.

- We can reduce our water consumption. Our wastewater finds its way into rivers, lakes and oceans and can spread diseases to marine animals and even damage whales' lungs.

- We can advocate for more funding to be granted to research projects that study the feeding zones used by whales. These studies would make it possible for us to regulate maritime traffic and take more effective measures to protect the places whales are known to travel. Cetaceans are like the tip of an iceberg—they are the most visible part of a marine ecosystem and can give us insight into the overall health of a much bigger world beneath the surface.

- As tourists, we can avoid going to shows at aquariums where people train and swim with dolphins and orcas. This can help reduce the hunting of these animals. Instead we can choose to observe cetaceans in their natural habitat by visiting places where the whale-watching industry is properly regulated. And most of all, we can change our expectations.

Together we can try to save these wonders of the natural world and teach ourselves new ways to look at the horizon. A whale's back cresting the water's surface might not seem like anything spectacular, but it is beautiful, simply because it means the whales are still here.

THANKS TO:

Marie-Sophie Giroux, previously the chief naturalist for the Group for Research and Education on Marine Mammals (GREMM) and now the partnering, engagement and communications officer for Parks Canada in the Saguenay–St. Lawrence Field Unit.

Patrice Corbeil, education director for the Group for Research and Education on Marine Mammals (GREMM), for his stories that are everything but concise.

Dominique Simard, for the stories and the myths, and for defending his little corner of paradise as fiercely as the Gauls resisted the Romans. By the way, he's given me permission to mention the name of his campground, because anyone who reads this far must really care about whales and nature. It's called Le Paradis Marin.

Jacques Gélineau, ecologist and environmentalist, for the extra information.

Chantal St-Hilaire, biologist, for raising my awareness.

France Boulianne, for the links and the welcome in Tadoussac.

Olivier Bernard, for his ability to translate scientific jargon for me.

Lucie Papineau, for believing in me and my book and encouraging me to make it look even more like what my heart told me it should be.

Martin Balthazar and the team at my original publisher, Les Éditions de la Bagnole, for being open to publishing this hybrid book and daring to do it.

Nathalie Dion, for illustrating the book of my dreams with such beautiful images and for sharing my vision and my passion. I wish these illustrations could have kept on coming!

RESOURCES

Discovery of Sound in the Sea, a University of Rhode Island website about the sounds cetaceans make and the issues of underwater noise: dosits.org

Fisheries and Oceans Canada (DFO), a federal institution that safeguards Canadian waters and manages Canada's fisheries and ocean resources. To report a dead whale, seal or other marine mammal or one in trouble, visit the website to find the correct contact information for your area: dfo-mpo.gc.ca/species-especes/mammals-mammiferes/report-rapport/page01-eng.html

Kavanagh, Ailbhe S. et al. "Evidence for the Functions of Surface-Active Behaviors in Humpback Whales (*Megaptera novaeangliae*)." *Marine Mammal Science* 33, no. 1 (November 21, 2016). onlinelibrary.wiley.com/doi/abs/10.1111/mms.12374

National Marine Life Center (NMLC), an independent, nonprofit organization that rehabilitates marine wildlife: nmlc.org

National Oceanic and Atmospheric Administration (NOAA) Fisheries, a US federal agency responsible for the management, conservation and protection of fish, marine life and their habitats. To report a stranded, injured or dead marine animal, visit the website to find the appropriate contact information for your region: fisheries.noaa.gov/report

Whales Online, a website created by the nonprofit Group for Research and Education on Marine Mammals (GREMM): baleinesendirect.org/en

INDEX